Refugees' Stories in Words, Paintings and Music

Out of Ira

Sybella Wilkes

Evans

Published by Evans Brothers Limited
2A Portman Mansions
Chiltern Street
London W1U 6NR
www.evansbooks.co.uk

Designer: Guy Callaby
Editor: Sonya Newland

British Library Cataloguing in Publication Data
Wilkes, Sybella.
Out of Iraq.
1. Refugees--Iraq--Juvenile literature.
2. Iraqis--Foreign countries--Juvenile literature.
3. Iraq--Social conditions--21st century--Juvenile literature.
I. Title
305.9'06914'09567-dc22

ISBN 9780237539306

Picture Credits
Michelle Alfaro/UNHCR: 20; **Bridgette Auger/UNHCR:** 12, 13, 14, 15, 18, 19, 21tr, 26, 27, 28, 29, 32, 36, 37, 38, 42, 43, 44, 45, 46, 47, 48, 49, 52, 53, 54, 55, 59, 61, 64, 65, 66, 68; **Gabriella Brust/UNHCR:** 1, 39, 50; **Corbis:** 8 (Sygma), 9 (Peter Turnley), 10 (Steve Raymer), 16 (Antoine Gyori/AGP), 17 (Christophe Calais), 22 (Reuters), 23 (epa), 33 (Hussein Al-Mousawi/epa); **Bassem Diab:** 11, 25, 31, 34, 35, 40, 41, 56, 58, 60, 62, 63, 67; **ECHO:** 69; **Getty Images:** 24; **Charles Lynch/UNHCR:** 21; **Ludi Lochner:** 7; **Refugees:** 30 (Fares), 51 (Shehab), 57 (Adam).

Sybella Wilkes would like to thank:
Dalia Al Achi, Michelle Alfaro, Bridgette Auger, Jeff Crisp, Rochelle Davis, Leo Dobbs, Paul Eedle, Leigh Foster, Mutassem Hayatla, Frauke Joosten Veglio, Laurens Jolles, Peter Kessler, Carole Laleve, Philippe Leclerc, Harb Mukhtar, Jeremy Paxman, Ron Redmond, Salwa Salti, Peter Stockholder

UNHCR has helped three Iraqi musicians, including Fadi Fares Aziz (pages 18–19) and Salim Salem (page 65) release their first album, *Transitions*. This can be downloaded from iTunes, Amazon and several other music-sharing sites. The musicians will donate the profits to a UNHCR-run financial-assistance programme that provides a lifeline for over 13,000 Iraqi refugee families unable to work legally in Syria.

Contents

Foreword

I was sitting down yesterday afternoon reading through this book and my 5 year old son crawled in my lap. He started to flip the pages and asked me questions. He would stop and look at the pages with children's drawings. He was enthralled by Shehab's story. He asked about him again before going to bed. I will keep Sybella's books in my children's room and, as they grow older and start asking more questions, I am comforted to know that this book will help give them some understanding.

She makes some of the most complicated subjects, such as war and displacement, easier to grasp. Somehow she has managed to write a book that is emotional and complex, but one that children are drawn to. I have been to both Syria and Iraq and visited refugee and internally displaced families from the conflict in Iraq, and nothing I could try to express

would come close to what this book accomplishes.

Refugee families are extraordinary. With this book, Sybella sheds light on their own unique voices. This is an important book. It gives us all a better understanding of

the lives of refugees and, with that, a better understanding of the world in general.

Angelina Jolie
UNHCR Goodwill Ambassador

Introduction

I arrived in Syria in September 2006 at the same time as hundreds of thousands of Iraqi refugees. As I dropped my children off at school I saw thousands queuing up outside the UN Refugee Agency (UNHCR) offices. When the opportunity came up to work with UNHCR, I took it immediately.

My first weeks were spent trying to figure out the situation in Iraq and the situation of Iraqi refugees. Unlike other refugee situations I had worked in in Africa, Iraqi refugees were not living in camps, but renting apartments in the capital Damascus and across the country. Most camps are terrible places and the only advantage is that you can reach the refugees easily and the refugees know how to reach UNHCR. UNHCR's challenge was to find the refugees, identify their needs and communicate these needs to a world that had closed its eyes to the consequences of the war in Iraq.

My first allies were Iraqi artists. Purely by chance I met a group of them, some of whom have told their stories in this book. Waleed's paintings of the bombing of the Samarra mosque tell a tragic story in a beautiful way. Salim Salem's music communicates centuries of musical experimentation with instruments that originate in Iraq and its neighbouring countries. Amr Ali's art communicates the pain of living with war for a peace-loving man. The painters and musicians have a well-deserved reputation that they have built up in Syria, and their exhibitions and concerts have packed audiences.

Past experience has taught me that refugee children tell the story of their lives in personal accounts and paintings in a manner that is often more eloquent and evocative than any politician can ever achieve. I compare the innocent art of my own children with the painful art of refugee children and I hope that these colourful yet sad reflections on refugee existence will help children and adolescents of the same age to relate to their lives.

This book is not a definitive guide to Iraq. It is a patchwork of accounts, paintings, recent historical events and photographs that leave the readers in a position to form their own opinions. Any discussion on war is going to be subjective. I have tried in this book to give the subject back to the Iraqis, who I believe are the best people to communicate about their lives and their country.

Sybella Wilkes

DEDICATION

This book is dedicated to Rick Hooper, who died along with 21 other colleagues working with the UN when the UN Building in Baghdad was bombed in August 2003. My husband Panos's best friend, Rick's entire career was committed to humanitarian work in the Middle East. We miss him terribly and continue to draw inspiration from our time spent together.

(See Attack on the United Nations, page 20)

Saddam: "he who confronts"

When Saddam Hussein (whose name means "he who confronts") became president of Iraq in 1979, he executed over 25 senior officials, many of whom had been his colleagues during his time as vice-president.

Saddam was leader of the Iraqi Baath party, which championed Arab unity and freedom from foreign control. The view that religion should not have a part in political or civic affairs was an important part of Baathism. However, Saddam used religion to advance his power.

As a member of the Sunni branch of Islam, Saddam always feared the influence of Iran over the Shiite population in Iraq. In both countries the majority are Shiite Muslims. One of Saddam's first actions when he became president was to go to war with Iran. He was supported in this by a number of Western and Middle Eastern countries, who wanted to undermine the power of Iran. Saddam hoped this war would gain him oil-rich land and

destabilise the Iranian leadership. He was mistaken. During the Iran-Iraq War, Saddam ordered the use of weapons such as mustard gas and nerve agents that killed thousands of people. His army had no choice but to follow his lethal orders – over 300 Iraqi officers were executed for opposing Saddam's tactics.

Within Iraq Saddam was ruthless in his efforts to quell opposition. During the war, many Kurdish Iraqis supported Iran, and Saddam ordered his cousin, Ali Hassan al-Majid (known as Chemical Ali), to lead an attack on the Kurds as punishment. The worst incident took place in

Right *Saddam Hussein addresses his troops during the Iran-Iraq War. Although many of them disagreed with the war, they had no choice but to obey his commands.*

"There's another way for the bloodshed to stop, and that is for the Iraqi military and the Iraqi people to take matters into their own hands to force Saddam Hussein, the dictator, to step aside."

US President George H. W. Bush, at the end of the Iran-Iraq War, 1991

the village of Halabja on 16–17 March 1988, when, according to human rights groups, chemical weapons killed between 3,200 and 5,000 people.

The Shiite population also suffered targeted suppression during Saddam's reign. A failed assassination attempt on Saddam in 1982 in the Shiite town of Dujail led him to take revenge on the village, executing 148 people. Saddam later survived seven other assassination attempts.

The First Gulf War

The Iran-Iraq War crippled Iraq's finances, and the situation was worsened by falling oil prices, because Iraq depended on the income from its oil. Saddam blamed Kuwait for this, believing that it was driving oil prices down by producing too much. His solution was to invade Kuwait in 1990 and claim the oil-rich territory for Iraq.

Countries all over the world imposed sanctions on Iraq, refusing to trade with it until Iraqi soldiers withdrew, but Saddam refused. The United Nations Security Council authorised "all necessary means to end the occupation". Over 32 countries sent troops to drive Iraqi forces out of Kuwait in what became known as the First Gulf War. This was successful, and by March 1991 Saddam's soldiers had left Kuwait.

More sanctions

Recent memory of the chemical attacks against Kurdish Iraqis, and worries over Iraq's capacity

Right An American soldier stands on a tank in Kuwait in 1991. Behind him, the oil fields are on fire.

to wage long-distance war on Israel and other countries, increased when UN weapons inspectors reported that Iraq was hiding much of its nuclear and chemical weapons programme.

UN Security Council sanctions on Iraq had devastating effects on the population. Malnutrition amongst children was widespread because there was not enough food, and many people died from preventable diseases because some medicines were not available. Saddam remained determined not to give in, and by 1998 some countries were

ready to give up on sanctions for the good of the Iraqi people.

On 15 December 1998, the UN chief weapons inspector, Richard Butler, reported that Iraq had failed to cooperate fully with weapons inspections. The following day, US President Bill Clinton announced that Saddam had "abused his last chance". The US and UK launched four days of air strikes called Operation Desert Fox, hoping to damage Iraq's weapon stores. For the next three years the US and UK bombed over 100 targets in Iraq.

9

Invasion

On 11 September 2001, terrorists attacked the World Trade Center and the Pentagon in the USA, killing nearly 3,000 people and shocking the world. No link has ever been established between Iraq and the people that carried out the 9/11 attacks, but the US response was to step up what it called "the war on terror", in particular against states it believed threatened US security. Iraq was top of this list.

Saddam Hussein denied being involved in the 9/11 attacks. Professing that Iraq did not have weapons of mass destruction, he allowed the weapons inspectors to return in November 2002, for the first time in four years. Unconvinced, President Bush approved a plan to send US troops to Iraq.

In January 2003, UN inspectors discovered 11 empty chemical warheads in Iraq that they had not been told about. The UN chief weapons inspector, Hans Blix, reported that, "Iraq appears not to have come to a genuine acceptance, not even today, of the disarmament that was demanded of it."

Arguments for and against war

While members of the UN Security Council questioned the wisdom of war, President Bush announced at the end of January that he was ready to go to war without the blessing of the UN. He was convinced that Iraq had chemical weapons that could be used against the US and other nations.

For a while, President Bush referred to those countries that supported the invasion of Iraq as the "Coalition of the Willing". The original list, prepared in March 2003, included 49 members. Of those, only four besides the US contributed troops to the invasion force (the UK, Australia, Poland and Denmark). Thirty-three provided some troops to support the occupation after the invasion was complete.

Left *Young people in Indiana, USA, protest against America's involvement in Iraq.*

In February 2003, the US, the UK and Spain made the case to the UN Security Council that it was time to use military force against Saddam's regime. France, Germany and Russia argued against going to war, recommending that weapons inspections be expanded to allow for "a real chance to the peaceful settlement of this crisis". Many of Iraq's neighbours expressed their opposition to war – they believed that military action should be a last resort.

Mission accomplished?

On 17 March, President Bush gave Saddam Hussein an ultimatum – leave Iraq within 48 hours or face invasion from the US and its supporters. Saddam did not respond to the ultimatum, so in the early hours of 20 March 2003, the US launched Operation Iraqi Freedom, backed up by the UK, Australia, Poland and Denmark. Described by President Bush as an "attack of opportunity" against targets in Iraq, the initial air strikes targeted Saddam Hussein and other Iraqi leaders. The coalition forces intended to combine air and ground assaults to defeat the Iraqis as quickly as possible. The Iraqi army was ill-equipped compared to the US and UK forces, and Saddam and his sons rapidly went into hiding. Within 21 days, the US-led forces had toppled the Iraqi government and captured the key cities in Iraq.

Above *War on the Streets, by Hassam Hadwani.*

"Let there be no misunderstanding: if Saddam Hussein does not fully disarm, for the safety of our people, and for the peace of the world, we will lead a coalition to disarm him."

US President George W. Bush

A life defined by war

Hussam (name changed) was born during the first Gulf War in 1991 and feels his whole life has been defined by one war or another in his country. He is still only a teenager, but his childhood was over a long time ago.

Above *Hussam grew up surrounded by the effects of war. Eventually he and his family were forced to leave Iraq and settle in Syria.*

●● My mother tells me the story of my birth like a horror story. It was 1991 and the war was approaching our city Baghdad and my mother was due to give birth. She took my sister to a village with no hospital, where a friend helped her give birth to me. There was no doctor or nurse there to notice that my hip was dislocated. Everyone was preoccupied with the war and there was no doctor to be found.

My parents are amazing people. My mother gave birth to me in such hardship, and throughout my childhood she always made the best of a bad situation. Once the war was over, the sanctions started. Overnight, money became meaningless. The Iraqi people were being punished for the political disagreement between our leader and others. Ordinary people did not count and our daily reminder was the struggle my mother had just to put food on the table.

Despite the hardship, my first six years in school were happy. I was surrounded by friends and we were able to be children. The invasion in 2003 changed everything. On 20 March we were all at school. By the evening the bombing of Baghdad had begun. I stayed at home, as did all my friends. On 9 April, Baghdad fell to the Americans.

The message went out, 'Return your children to school, return to work.' When I returned to school, my classroom was half empty. This story happened over and over again. Safety won over education.

My father believed that my education was more important than anything. It would keep me safe in the future. But even we had to make compromises. I changed school to one closer to the house. I was no safer there, though, and we faced the terror of a foreign army entering our school. One day we were told that there was a booby-trapped car outside our school. It was very scary.

Outside the school was a patch of land that seemed to attract horror. One day dead bodies were left there. Another day, when I was in the middle of an exam, all the windows broke after there was an explosion on that piece of land. Several days later, the land was in use again by the militia launching rockets.

Despite all this, my parents made sure that my sisters and I went to school. My father would walk me to school; my mother would be with my sisters. My father was spending more and more time at home. As a lawyer living in an increasingly lawless country, his work became dangerous. We heard reports of lawyers being murdered for choosing to defend a particular person. My father explained that the war in Iraq gave every man with a grudge the excuse to take his revenge without fear of reprisal. It infected every part of our lives. At school a student who failed his class could threaten his teacher.

Despite the hardship, my first six years in school were happy. The invasion in 2003 changed everything.

It came as no surprise, then, when my father was targeted. First he was attacked on the street while in his car. Then the attackers came to our house and he was severely beaten. Lastly the militia fired into our house. Luckily our house was huge so we could escape the bullets. It was clear my father had to leave. With him in Syria, I was now the man of the house.

We reasoned that my sisters, mother and I could stay in Iraq. Who would want to hurt us? We no longer felt safe at home, but my parents were adamant we should continue school. For most of 2005 we spent the year moving from one relative to the next, but we continued going to school. Then 2006 struck and we started doubting our safety. Down the street a woman and her child were killed. A mad man with a rocket launcher seemed to be spending a lot of time on our street.

In the summer of 2006 we left for Syria. We found my father living

in a tiny house, a fraction of the size of our home. If we had been shot at in this house, there would have been nowhere to hide!

Throughout 2007 I worked to help my family, helping out in restaurants and at weddings. I gave up school for some time. Now I am back at school and just work at weekends and during

holidays. It means there is less money at home, but my mother keeps smiling and tells me that she has always been good at managing on very little. ❞

Below Hussam's sister holds up a picture of their old kitchen – a stark comparison to the one in their new home in Syria.

Flight: a child's memory of invasion

Ahmed's father is a religious imam. He and his family are waiting in Syria until they can return to Iraq. They were offered resettlement to Europe, but decided that their ties to Iraq were too important, so they took the risk of turning down this opportunity in the hope that they would one day be able to return to Iraq. With a lot of encouragement from his visiting relatives, he told his story.

●● I have a strong memory of my beautiful house with its nice garden. We had a good life in Iraq. My father was the imam of the mosque, a pillar of the community. I can still picture the garden, with my bike there. My friends Hamadeh and Osthman lived nearby, always ready to play football or go for a bicycle ride.

My simple, peaceful life ended abruptly when my father was targeted. In a single day, 37 imams like him were killed. Soon afterwards, he was driving home and men fired at him. We did not want to leave our home; we stayed even though a simple visit to the market with my father often involved gunfire and the sounds of rockets. After a while my mother would not let me out of the house, not even to the garden. My friends were not there any more. Our bicycle tyres deflated because we never used our bicycles.

Television announcements warned us that life was about to get worse. Store water, buy food, be ready to move at any time, we were told. We did this, but never really imagined that we would have to leave home.

And then that day came when we had to leave. My parents decided that we would die if we stayed at home. We piled all the food and water we had saved into the car, and blankets and mattresses on the roof. No space for my toys.

It was pouring with rain when we left. It was hard to differentiate the sound of lightning, thunder and gunfire. Ahead of us the road was bombarded – destroyed – so we had to turn around again and find another route out. By the time we arrived at the village outside Baghdad, the blankets and mattresses were soaked through. I could only remember my nice bedroom at home.

We stayed in a house with eight other families. There was always a long queue for the bathroom. In this new home, my father was no longer the imam. It was so hard living in that house and one day we decided to risk going home.

It was a risk that we kept repeating, but then my father escaped an assassination attempt and it really was time to go again – this time to Syria.

We took a taxi, filled it with our things. Still no space for my toys. I found myself in a new country, away from my beautiful Iraq.

Soon after we arrived we heard the worst of all news. My sister's new husband had been killed. She ran away when armed men came, but they set our house on fire and left. My poor sister had to follow us, and now we all live together, waiting to return. I am old enough now to know it is not safe. 'Not yet,' my father says. 'Maybe next year it will be safe to return.' ❞

Destruction Behind Closed Doors

The Iraqi insurgency began as soon as the invasion started. At first the resistance came from those who were loyal to Saddam Hussein, but soon others became angry at the occupation of Iraq, particularly religious radicals. Known as "anti-Iraqi forces", initially they targeted the coalition troops and anyone in Iraq they believed was helping Western governments. Gradually the violence spread, as rival religious groups – the Shiite and Sunni Muslims – waged war against each other for power and revenge. Civilians were the worst affected by the insurgency. The insurgents practised guerilla warfare and often targeted people for no other reason than that certain leaders had a personal problem with their politics or beliefs.

British soldiers arrest a member of an Iraqi militia on the road to Basra in April 2003.

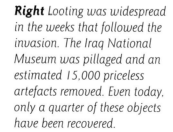

Right *Looting was widespread in the weeks that followed the invasion. The Iraq National Museum was pillaged and an estimated 15,000 priceless artefacts removed. Even today, only a quarter of these objects have been recovered.*

Who's in charge?

On 22 May 2003, the UN Security Council passed a resolution that ended the sanctions against Iraq. The US and the UK effectively became the country's occupying powers, when a body called the Coalition Provisional Authority was established to provide leadership in Iraq until a democratically elected parliament could take over.

Although there were many international troops ready to take part in the invasion of Iraq, a number of these did not see combat and were withdrawn after the invasion was successful. As it turned out, perhaps it would have been better to have left more soldiers in the region – they would be needed to maintain law and order as fighting broke out between groups of Iraqis.

In the weeks following the invasion of Iraq, many places were looted, including the Iraq National Museum and Saddam's main palace.

Such behaviour highlighted one of the biggest problems Iraq would face in the months and years to come. Although coalition forces had wanted to free Iraq from Saddam's dictatorship, the invasion had left no Iraqi authority in charge. This provided opportunity for militant groups, criminals and foreign fighters to exploit the situation for their own ends.

Music among the bombs

A nai (flute) player, Fadi Fares Aziz was studying music at the University of Baghdad when the invasion of Iraq took place. Despite all the danger and disruption, he was determined to complete his education.

❝❞ A few months after I started at university to study music the war began. My faculty was closed and I fled with my family to a small village to wait out the war. I took my flute with me and tried to keep my mind on music rather than bombs. As soon as I heard that professors were returning to the university, I too returned to Baghdad to check out the situation. Every day brought news of classmates who had been killed.

While lawlessness seemed to be raging outside – the museum was being pillaged – I decided to concentrate on my music. My teachers were so inspiring. My classmates and I felt an obligation to work like normal. We were not prepared to throw away this opportunity. After all, we were the 150 lucky students who had been selected out of thousands of candidates to study at the university.

Take a moment to think about what I had to face on each journey to university. The military, militia, police, US troops … they would all stop the bus for no reason. Sometimes for 10 minutes, sometimes for 30 minutes. The first few days I was scared, but it became a routine. Some days the entire road would be closed with barriers and we would have to walk through fields to reach another road.

Right *Now he is a refugee, Fadi sees his flute and the music he plays as links to his homeland of Iraq.*

My flute case looked too much like a gun case, so I had to find another way of carrying it. First I used a rice bag, but I still worried about the shape making people suspicious. Then I heard about a new technique to cut the flute into pieces. I had my flute cut up and I would carry it in pieces and fit it back together at the university.

Attending university was such an effort. A journey that used to take me 30 minutes now took up to two hours to achieve. Once there, every lesson, every practice, had to count. If the journey was not enough, the very act of practising music soon became dangerous. My faculty started receiving threats that said, 'Close! Your work is *haram* (against God).' The building I studied in was attacked, and all the glass was shattered.

My flute case looked too much like a gun case, so I had to find another way of carrying it.

Above *Fadi had his flute cut up into two pieces so that he could travel across Baghdad without causing suspicion that his instrument was a gun.*

I think it was more stressful for my parents than for me. They would wait at home, worrying. One day I was very late home because I was on the bus in the area where the militia and US troops were fighting. On two other occasions home-made bombs were planted next to US checkpoints at the same time

I was in the area. During three years I witnessed six explosions. I am so lucky I was never hurt. The worry became too much for my parents after they heard that on two occasions men wearing camouflage uniform had boarded the bus I was travelling on. The second time this happened, a group of young men on the bus

were taken away. I still wonder what happened to them.

I graduated from university and was offered a teaching position there. I would have loved to have stayed, but my parents did not want to take the risk. I packed my flute and came to Syria.

My flute is my link with Iraq. It is an essential part of an Iraqi music ensemble. The nature of the instrument is to reflect sadness and longing. My favourite piece is called 'The Night in Baghdad', which evokes the beautiful evenings in Baghdad before the war.

Today I am barely surviving. For the first year I played at a nightclub to earn money. After a year I was exhausted and my inspiration was bleeding out of me. Last year thousands of Iraqis left Iraq after hanging on for more than five years. This gave me a sense of hopelessness, that this period of waiting to reclaim my life is not going to end any time soon. ●●

Attack on the United Nations

On 19 August 2003, a cement truck laden with explosives detonated right outside the United Nations offices in Baghdad. Twenty-two people were killed and more than 150 were wounded. Amongst them were the top United Nations envoy in Iraq, Sergio Vieira de Mello, and 21 UN workers, all dedicated to humanitarian work in Iraq.

After this attack, many humanitarian workers withdrew from Iraq since it was too dangerous to work there, while dedicated Iraqi staff worked from home. It would take five years before the UN considered the environment safe enough to return in any strength.

Michelle Alfaro was appointed Protection Officer with the Iraq office of the United Nations High Commissioner for Refugees (UNHCR) in 2005, when Iraq was considered too dangerous for humanitarian agencies to base their staff inside Iraq. She was based in Jordan, and every trip into Iraq had to be planned with military support from international forces.

❝ While Iraqis were waging war on one another and with the multinational forces, UNHCR still had a responsibility for the refugees from other countries trapped in the middle of the violence. One of my first trips into central Iraq was in September 2006. I first had to fly into Baghdad, then take a helicopter into another part of Iraq and then wait for another military helicopter to Anbar

One of the soldiers pointed out a man lying under a truck watching us with binoculars. It was time to go.

province in the west, where a camp of Sudanese refugees was located. Even though some had lived for up to 15 years in Iraq, they were threatened simply because they were different and foreign. It took us two days to get to the camp. We finally arrived at a military base, exhausted. It felt weird to be surrounded by the military on my first humanitarian mission into central Iraq.

The next day we were taken to the camp by military convoy. Before leaving I had to put on a heavy flak jacket and UN helmet

that we covered with camouflage so that the local insurgents would not know that the refugees had been meeting with the UN. When I stepped off the vehicle I was greeted by the refugees wearing just shirts for protection. They were so pleased to see us and relieved that we were finally able to visit them so they could tell us about their experiences and ask us for help.

The refugees were living in a very difficult situation. On one side was a gas station frequented by militants. Further down the road was the base of the multinational forces. The refugees had to negotiate their way between the two sides. The bullet holes in their tents and burned vehicles were testament to the number of times that their camp was in the wrong place at the wrong time.

The soldiers that accompanied me were really concerned about the refugees. They wanted to help them to get out. Every tent was lined with the boxes of the ready-made meals that the soldiers gave the refugees.

Many of the refugees had children. I was in the middle of talking

with some of their mothers to understand the difficulty of the situation, when one of the soldiers accompanying me pointed out a man lying under a truck watching us with binoculars. It was time to go. The refugees were left to negotiate their safety again, unwatched and unprotected. I left the camp promising to spread the word about their

Left UNHCR worker Michelle Alfaro with refugees in central Iraq.

Above Michelle meeting with a group of Palestinian refugee women, who fled the violence in Iraq and are currently living in Al Hol refugee camp in northern Syria.

situation. That was all the refugees asked of me. At the beginning of 2009 the last of the refugees from the camp were finally evacuated to Romania, where they are waiting to be processed for resettlement applications to the US. I am so relieved that they are finally safe. 99

Saddam and his family

Saddam's two sons, Uday and Qusay, were deeply involved in the dark side of their father's control of Iraq. Uday fell from grace after his excesses became embarrassing even by Saddam's standards. He had Uday imprisoned after he killed his personal valet. With time Saddam relented and gave Uday more responsibility, which included heading the Olympic Committee, supervising various Iraqi media outlets and overseeing the Fedayeen Saddam – a band of armed militants, mostly ex-convicts, that eventually became part of Saddam's security service. Qusay was gradually elevated by Saddam until he was leading the Republican Guard, the most important military division in Iraq.

Right Saddam Hussein with his two sons, Uday (left) and Qusay (right).

Saddam's sons

Both sons killed many times. Qusay killed to please his father and further his career. He was given the task of crushing the Shiite uprising after the first Gulf War. Hundreds of Shiites were detained and, according to eye witnesses, Qusay personally executed four prisoners before ordering the execution of several hundred others.

For Uday, torture was a hobby. He kept a private torture chamber, disguised as an electricity installation and known as the Red Room, in a building on the banks of the Tigris River. Amongst others, the entire national football team was repeatedly tortured, notably when it failed to qualify for the 1994 World Cup. As part of their torture, members of the team were forced to kick concrete footballs. No woman was safe with Uday, and there are countless stories of abductions and rapes. Uday and

Qusay killed to please his father and further his career. For Uday, torture was a hobby.

Qusay were killed during a huge gunfight while resisting arrest by US forces on 22 July 2003, in the northern Iraqi city of Mosul.

Victims within the family

While some members of Saddam's family were involved in acts of persecution, others were victims. A cousin of Saddam, Ala Abd Al-Qadir Al-Majid, fled to Jordan from Iraq, citing problems with the regime. His return to Iraq was well-publicised, with the Iraqi ambassador in Jordan giving public assurances that he could return to Iraq without any threat to his life. He was met at the border by the head of Iraq's intelligence agency (the *Mukhabarat*), Tahir Habbush, who took him to a farm where other family members waited for him. At the farm he was tied to a tree and members of his immediate family – under orders from Saddam – took it in turns to shoot him.

Some 40 of Saddam's relatives, including women and children, were killed on orders from

Saddam. His sons-in-law, Hussein Kamel and Saddam, had defected with their wives and children in 1995, fearing for their lives. They returned to Iraq after the government had announced amnesties for them. The amnesties proved false, and after swift divorces from Saddam's daughters, the men were shot by Saddam's security forces in 1996.

Saddam captured

After months of a manhunt, in which a US$25 million reward was offered for information that led to Saddam's capture, he was

Above *Saddam, shortly after his capture in 2003. Following a trial on counts of war crimes, crimes against humanity and genocide, he was executed by hanging during the morning prayer on 30 December 2006.*

finally caught in a hole in the ground, with only enough space to lie down while he hid from US troops. His first words to soldiers when he was captured were in English. He said: "I am Saddam Hussein. I am the President of Iraq and I want to negotiate." The response of the US troops who pulled him out of his hiding hole was: "President Bush sends his regards."

Anarchy, Kidnapping and Civil War

Although violence was already a considerable problem, the bombing of the important Shiite shrine, the Askariya mosque, by Sunni Muslims in February 2006 unleashed screams of rage and revenge from the Shiite community, which were matched in ferocity by their Sunni neighbours. This bombing marked the beginning of civil war.

Right *The bombing of one of Iraq's most important Shiite shrines, the Askariya mosque in Samarra, left the famous golden dome in ruins.*

Civilians became the prime targets. In some cases, religious disagreements were used as justification for Sunni and Shiite militias targeting each other in suicide bombings, assassinations, abductions and executions. In other cases the militia made the most of the lack of security to earn huge sums of money from families by kidnapping and other criminal activities. Everyone was targeted – civilians and soldiers, young and old, rich and poor, educated and uneducated. The height of the violence was in Baghdad, although many other cities, towns and villages were also badly affected. Worst affected were areas that were home to people from different religious, ethnic and educational backgrounds. Religious minorities were particularly vulnerable.

SUNNI–SHIITE SPLIT
This split in Islam dates back to disputes over the successor to the Prophet Mohammed nearly 1,400 years ago. Many Muslims, including Iraqi Muslims, choose not to be identified as either, since they consider this to be a private matter. All Muslims believe that there is one god, Allah.

Below *A painting by an Iraqi girl, Aya Mohamed Selman, called* The Day of Invasion.

"This is as 9/11 in the United States."

Adel Abdul Mahdi, one of Iraq's two Vice-Presidents, 2006

"If the government's security forces cannot provide the necessary protection, the believers will do it."

Grand Ayatollah Ali al-Sistani, Iraq's most senior Shiite cleric

Just as devastating was the breakdown of basic services, such as electricity, safe water supplies and even fuel. Some estimates at the time found that over one-third of Iraq's doctors left. For those that stayed, medical supplies were scarce and a number of killings in hospitals in Baghdad left patients terrified to stay in hospital.

Professionals and educated people who chose a more moderate lifestyle (not necessarily according to any religious doctrine) were targeted with a vengeance. Threats drove them from their work, homes, schools and families. Many became refugees for the first time in their lives.

A family in fear

Iraqi journalist Maysoon explains how she and her family were driven from their home because of her job.

Left Journalist Maysoon was driven out of Iraq and now lives in Syria with her husband and three sons.

Right Maysoon's son Omar, now 17, had to leave school three years ago to work. He washes cars on the streets to help support his family.

●● Yesterday my youngest son, Hussein, woke up and came to lie next to me. 'Don't go back, Mummy,' he said. 'Next time they will kill you.' He is only six, but has seen so much.

He was at home sleeping when a group of men came to the house to try and take away my husband. We had been dreading this. At the newspaper where my husband worked, one by one people had left after they were threatened, until he was the only Sunni person at work. My eldest son, Ali, was at home and we thank God that he was able to help defend his father. The men hit my husband over the head with a pistol. My husband kept staggering back up, covered in blood. The only reason they didn't use the gun was they

26

didn't want to be heard by the nearby military forces. I knew that I had to scream and scream to let the world know what was happening. The men left as quickly as they came. Hussein awoke with the screams and I hope he forgets the vision of his family distraught after that attack.

I knew that I had to scream and scream to let the world know what was happening.

My husband did not go back to work. All around him he heard about people being kidnapped or killed, and he felt that he could not trust anyone at work. Several neighbours said that I should also stop working, but how would we live? We did not want to leave Iraq for certain poverty.

I was approached about a new job with an Iraqi television station. We took this as a sign that life was going to start getting better for us. As I was leaving training in my first week, two men attacked me on the street. I screamed and screamed, wondering if any of my colleagues would hear me. I was saved by

chance. An Iraqi military patrol came around the corner. The two men jumped back in their car, but yelled at me, 'We will follow you again, Maysoon. You will never be safe here.' I couldn't consider going back to that place. Would I have the courage to stand in front of the television camera and make myself and my family even more vulnerable?

At the same time my middle son, Omar, was threatened at school. I always loved the name Omar, but it turns out that this is a Sunni name. On the news we heard that a militia group was offering US$1,000 for every Omar caught. His classmates taunted him saying, 'You are worth a thousand dollars.' After several days of taunts he could not face school any more. How I regretted the names of my children. We named our first son Ali and it turns out that Ali is a classic Shiite name. I chose the name because I liked it, but Ali was going to a Sunni school in our

neighbourhood and was taunted by his classmates that he came from a mixed marriage. We were unsafe everywhere.

So, two weeks after I was attacked we packed a couple of bags and left for Syria. We did not tell anyone except my mother. We arrived in Syria with just enough money to pay the first month's rent. Shortly after we left my mother said that people were looking for us. A threatening letter with a bullet in it arrived at our house.

Right *Youngest son Hussein shows one of the threatening letters the family received.*

Our little Hussein rarely leaves the house, now. What if he gets in trouble too? I don't want to take any risks. I don't send him to school. I can't face it. I don't want my last son to face any problems. This untouched child is the future for me. He deserves a good future. **❞**

Waleed's story

Waleed is an Iraqi artist. He fled to Turkey after the bombing at Samarra when he was threatened. He explains how he fled Baghdad – and how he longs to return.

●● When the dictator, Saddam, was eliminated I felt so optimistic that Iraq could become a country of love and peace. But the invasion of Iraq led to a whole new war starting, a war I describe as a 'settling of accounts' among different religions and political groups that came from outside Iraq.

There were too many groups to mention them all by name. For me the most dangerous were those that wanted to turn Iraq into a place that suited their extreme view of religion. They saw Iraq as a capital of Islam. This new enemy had vicious plans that aimed to divide Iraqis. In order to achieve their aim, they targeted holy shrines. The most devastating was the Golden Dome of Samarra, because they knew how important this is to the Shiite people. They exploded the dome. From this moment, the game started. Many sacred shrines and sites were targeted, both Sunni and Shiite. Sunni and Shiite clerics were targeted. Places of worship became religious courts. They hid arms depots and factories of bombs that killed Iraqis every day as they did their shopping in markets. My beloved Baghdad became a horrible place to live.

In order to live in Baghdad you had to change your identity or ethnic affiliation all the time. One day you were Sunni. The next Shiite. Why? Because fake checkpoints would stop your car and ask about the identity and faith of the passengers. All my friends hold two identity cards: Sunni and Shiite! It shows how unimportant it actually is.

Left *Waleed's painting shows the bombing of the shrine of Samarra. This event was the turning point for many Iraqis, who felt they could no longer stay in their homeland.*

Right *Waleed displays his paintings, which reflect his feelings on events in his country and life as a refugee.*

The war exhausted my spirit, and I knew that it was too much of a risk to stay in Iraq. I took a very quick decision to leave Iraq. I went to Turkey first, where I exhibited my art, and then to Syria, where the United Nations held an exhibition of my work. These exhibitions allowed me to express my feelings about the destruction taking place in Iraq.

I left Iraq because of the nightmare of violence. Now I am haunted by the nightmare of waiting. I suffer from homesickness. I feel like a tree that has been stolen from its land, but whose roots are still in Iraq. ●●

Waleed has now been resettled to the US and held his first exhibition in New York in 2009.

"I feel like a tree that has been stolen from its land, but whose roots are still in Iraq."

Abduction

Fares (name changed) remembers the terror of the night he was kidnapped by a militia group. His life and that of his family were threatened, and he feels lucky to have survived.

Left *Fares took this photograph to represent the dark corridor his life became during his abduction. After spending two years in Syria he has now returned to Iraq, where he is studying Computer Engineering.*

●● The day I was abducted, I had been sent by my mother to buy bread for dinner. My mother told me to go quickly because it was 6.30 in the evening. When I walked around the corner of the street there was a black BMW parked with four men in it, all wearing black masks. The man next to the driver pointed a gun at me while the other two came out of the car and caught hold of me. I was frozen. They tied my hands together, covered my eyes and told me that if I made a sound they would kill me.

We travelled in silence for 10 minutes, maybe less, then I was

I could see no sign of light from the space under my blindfold. I never thought that silence could be so frightening.

led out of the car into a room. They didn't speak to me, just led me into the room. As I heard the door close I felt absolute darkness around me. I could see no sign of light from the space under my blindfold. I never thought that silence could be so frightening.

After perhaps an hour, two men walked in and started asking me questions. I had not told them my name, but they knew it. The first question was, 'Fares, why are you and your Sunni family living in a Shiite area?' I answered that I had lived there all my life, and considered the area to be my home. I reminded them that I was a child and I lived where my family was. There followed another long silence. I didn't know if the men were still there or if they had gone. After 15

minutes they asked me, 'Why don't you move to a Sunni area?' I told them that I couldn't throw away 15 years of my life, that my school, home and family were all in this area and we did not know anywhere else to live. I was left for a long time in silence. Then out of the silence came the question, 'What do you think, shall I kill you or shall I release you?' I had prepared myself for this question and I told them, 'It depends on God's will. If I am to die today it is my destiny.'

After this question I was left standing in the dark, wondering about my destiny for what felt like an hour. Then the men took me back to the car, where they told me that I should deliver a warning to my family. We had two choices – move to another area and stay alive, or stay in the area and get killed. The car stopped and the men guided me out. They cut the ties on my hands and told me to stand and wait for five minutes before removing the blindfold. It was difficult to judge how long five minutes was, but after a while I took off the blindfold and found that I was in the same place they had taken me from. I paused for a moment to look at my hands and body and thank God that I was alive. As I ran home I thanked God again and again. ●●

A family divided

Nine-year-old Nabil (name changed) tells the story of how his family has been torn apart because his parents come from different religious backgrounds.

●● We are a family living under pressure. I was a small boy when we left Iraq, but even so, I was old enough to remember gunfights on my street and near my home. Back at home there was another fight going on. I honestly didn't know what the problem was, but it all surrounded the words Sunni and Shiite. It seems that my father is one, my mother the other. This was not a problem when they married, but it became a problem for my mother's family.

The louder the gunfire, the more the problems increased, until one day my father decided it was time for us to leave. I was leaving a big house, full of my mother's family – my grandfather, my aunts, my cousins. And here I am, in Syria.

We live a quiet life. In the same room that we sleep, my father paints his paintings. Our home is furnished with mattresses and blankets the UN gave us. My father is hesitant to invite people home. Home is just one room, with a bathroom and a kitchen across a courtyard. My parents remind us that they love us and we know they love each other. It is hard to be away from Iraq, but my father says that we cannot live there while there is so much pressure from the family. ●●

Right Nabil's artist father, Ahmed, now paints in the family's tiny home in Syria.

31

Becoming a Refugee

By 2007, after three and a half years of nearly constant warfare, hundreds of thousands of Iraqi refugees moved to neighbouring countries, including Syria, Jordan, Lebanon and Egypt. Many escaped with just their lives, leaving behind all their possessions. Most had lost friends and relatives to the violence, kidnapping and insecurity in Iraq.

"This is one of the biggest movements of displaced people in the Middle East since the Palestinian crisis in 1948."

UNHCR High Commissioner António Guterres, Amman, Jordan, February 2007

When they arrived in their new country the refugees had to find somewhere to live and a way of earning a living. In most host countries, refugees were not allowed to work. If any of them had been lucky enough to escape with some savings, these were quickly used up on rent, food and simply surviving from day to day. As time went on, refugees resorted to desperate means to survive. Children were obliged to work, families were evicted from homes because they could not afford the rent. Many had to call on friends and family in Iraq and overseas to help them make ends meet.

Right *Iraqi refugees in Syria wait to be registered at the UNHCR centre in Damascus.*

The largest numbers of refugees went to Syria and Jordan, creating considerable pressure on local services, schools and the security of neighbourhoods where refugees settled. In Syria the government set the tone, describing the refugees as "guests" or "visitors". Until October 2007 the borders were open to Iraqis fleeing for their lives. For several months in 2007, at least 3,000 Iraqis a day arrived in Syria.

Poor countries themselves, both Syria and Jordan appealed for help. By 2008, Western governments had committed tens of millions of dollars to support Iraqi refugees, but this still did not meet the needs of so many refugees living in such extreme poverty.

In addition to the refugees, a similar number of Iraqis fled to other parts of Iraq. At the height of the crisis it was estimated that over four million Iraqis had become refugees or internally displaced in Iraq.

UNHCR tents at a camp for internally displaced persons at Najaf. Despite international aid, Iraqis driven from their homes suffer shortages of food and clean water.

A childhood in chaos

Adam's (name changed) school years were defined by a war that was not being fought miles away, but right on his doorstep. One day it even spilled into his classroom.

●● The war started in Iraq during my sixth grade. While the aeroplanes were bombing the city I was just a little boy studying as hard as I could to succeed in my exams. These exams were so important. I needed over 95 per cent to get into Baghdad College, arguably the best school in Iraq, and I did not allow the chaos around me to distract me from this ambition.

I thought these exams would be the greatest challenge of my life, but actually attending school became my greatest challenge. The security situation was bad and my parents were constantly worrying about me getting hurt on the long journey to school or at school itself. There was a police station near my school that was waging war against militia groups in the area.

One day the militia won the battle and took over the police station. We heard the news in our classrooms and were told to hide under our desks. We wanted to go to the bomb shelter, but the headmaster had the key and he was unable to get back to the school. The next thing we knew, there were helicopters right over

Left and Right *Paintings by Iraqi children Hassan Izaldeen (Packing) and Aya Mohamed Selman (Immigration).*

the school with machine guns firing. I'm sure they were trying to fire at the police station, but our school was so close it was hard to miss. One of my classmates was hit with a bullet in his leg.

Every morning my parents had to make the decision about whether or not my brother and I should go to school. They would listen to the news, call friends, receive calls from friends, and all this time we would be dressed and ready to go, ready to stay. Once we made our decision, we did not change our minds. That was our rule. One day we made the wrong decision. We had the bad luck to pass a military checkpoint at the same time it was being attacked. The car was hit by bullets from the attackers and the military firing back. We were so lucky no one was hurt because bullets hit the front of our car.

By 2006 we were only taking the chance of going to school three days out of five. The pressure

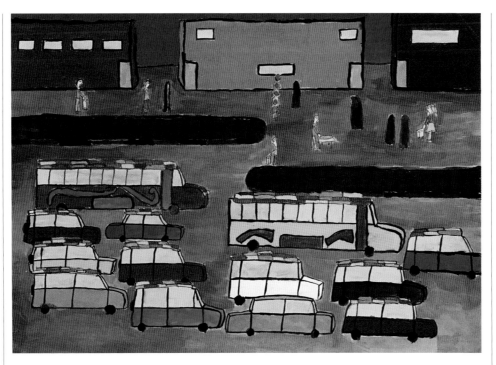

was on my brother, Omar, who needed to study hard to succeed in his exams if he was going to join me at Baghdad College. At the end of his exams one day my father was held up at one of the many checkpoints, so Omar found himself waiting outside his school alone. Some men approached him and addressed him by name. They told him that

One of my classmates was hit with a bullet in his leg.

my father had sent them to pick him up. He was scared because he didn't recognise them. Just then my father arrived. Omar ran for the car. As he ran one of the men fired into the air. Omar collapsed in fear, unable to move, despite my father's calls. My father left his car, ran to Omar and carried him back to the car, with bullets now aimed at them. They drove back home, my brother totally traumatised. We think that these men were trying

to take Omar as part of a campaign by a militia group to capture and kill boys and men with the name of Omar.

He did not want to go back to school, but my father wanted him to finish his exams. I am so proud of my brother that he sat his last exams. After this attempt to take him, my poor brother became scared of his own name. He was scared to leave the house; some days he did not even want to get out of bed. When my parents named him Omar, no one would have said that this was a dangerous name. I was lucky, I have a name that crosses the religious divide between Sunni and Shiite. ❥❥

Adam, age 17, is the name chosen by this student, since he is worried about his story following him in his future, when he may want to forget his bad memories of Iraq. His story continues on page 46, and he shows a photo essay on his friend Mustafa on page 57.

An artist in exile

Amr Ali is an artist. He fled to Syria after he was accused of supporting Saddam Hussein and later helping the Americans. Although he misses his home, he has no wish to return while life is so dangerous for a peace-loving artist.

●● My life has been defined by wars and armies that I have done my best to avoid. I grew up at a time when every boy expected to enter the army. War was waging with Iran, there were attacks on Iraqi people throughout the country. After finishing school I entered the Baghdad school of Fine Arts. I was never free and was often obliged to paint portraits of Saddam Hussein. For me my art is all about expressing the way I feel, and that was a dangerous way of living one's life under Saddam. So from the moment that I graduated my focus has always been on finding ways out of Iraq.

I paid my way out of national service by selling paintings. Once I had the necessary papers, my focus was then on getting to know the rest of the world. My only option was to visit Syria and Jordan, where I was able to get a visa. At the end of 1999 I had made a good sum of money in Jordan, enough to finally marry the woman I loved. I felt ready to return to Iraq to make my future with her. I don't even want to describe the disaster that happened during the journey home, but suffice it to say that all the money was stolen and I returned to Iraq penniless and obliged to end my engagement.

Over the next couple of years I travelled in and out of Syria frequently. I was there when Saddam's regime fell. I decided to wait to see what would happen, but after a couple of months I was ready to go back to Baghdad. For the first time I felt free in

Baghdad. Before the fall of Saddam we were not able to use mobile phones or the Internet. Overnight our horizons expanded dramatically. I felt light of spirit and felt that my life no longer had to focus on escaping Iraq. There was plenty of opportunity, particularly with the US military. One day I was travelling to visit the soldiers with some partly finished work to show them.

Above and Right
Amr Ali's paintings reflect his feelings about the events that have happened in his country, and about how it feels to be a refugee, having to live in a country far from home.

From the moment that I graduated my focus has always been on finding ways out of Iraq.

Militias stopped my car and, seeing my art, threatened me. I still shudder to remember that gun pointed at me. I was told in no uncertain terms that I should either stop painting for the foreigners or I would be killed. From that time on I started noticing the world closing in around me – the brave new Iraq disappearing in front of me.

One day the violence reached my doorstep. Masked men came to my home when only my father was there. He does not know who they were, but it is clear that they knew me well enough to

know that I had decorated the local offices with Saddam's portraits during the 1990s. After treating my father roughly, they proceeded to his supermarket and set it on fire. My family could no longer face the threat to our lives. We joined the tens of thousands of peace-loving Iraqis who packed their bags to go to Syria.

In Syria I had to start selling my work to support my family. I was living in shock and my art was my only release. I painted a dark picture of my family crossing the border into Syria, memories of gangs in the streets and flashback memories of my life in Iraq. Some of my art sold, but many people don't want war in their homes. I can't blame them. I have done my best to avoid war myself. I cannot pretend that life has been easy. I have faced many disappointments but at least I am free to paint what I like. I try

Left *Amr Ali now runs art classes for refugee children in Syria.*

Right *Amr Ali called this painting* Angels.

to keep a low profile, but at the same time it is important that my name as an artist is known.

I plan to marry soon. I hope that my new wife and I can live a long way away, where I can forget the violence of Iraq and see the world as a good place again. I cannot face the thought of Iraq for now. I dream of emigrating somewhere else. ❞

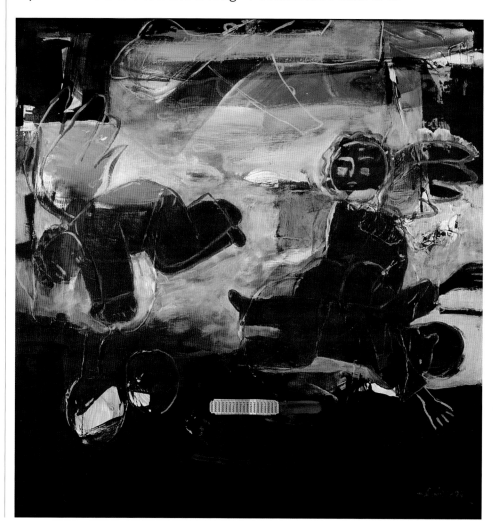

Helping refugees

Oula Ramadan is a Syrian working as a registration clerk with the UN Refugee Agency (UNHCR). She interviews up to seven families a day, records their stories and ensures they are directed to the help they need.

Right Oula hopes that by helping Iraqi refugees in Syria they will have a chance to regain their sense of safety and happiness.

Above As a worker for UNHCR, Oula has met hundreds of Iraqi families every year who have fled their country.

❝ Nothing in my life has prepared me for this job. My day starts and ends with human suffering. For the first months I was in shock at the terrible accounts I was hearing every day: murder, torture, kidnapping, death and separation. Even my worst dreams could not have included the situations that Iraqis described daily to me.

I feel incredibly motivated by my work. I need courage for my job. This courage also comes from the Iraqi families I meet. When they walk into the interview booth, they are always well-presented, dignified and strong. No one could imagine the stories they have to tell.

I am very careful to spare children from the worst details of their parents' suffering.

The smiles on their faces hide the terrible suffering they have in their souls.

Many of my interviews involve children. I am very careful to spare children from hearing the worst details of their parents' suffering. We have a playroom provided by UNICEF with Red Crescent volunteers who are ready to play with the children while their parents tell their stories. While I have a task to do, and my supervisors make sure I do it, I consider it my personal responsibility to go beyond this task. For every family that tells me that their children are not going to school, I urge them to reconsider. 'Life is long. They should go to school. It is free in Syria,' I tell them. Many of the Iraqi children I have interviewed are coping with problems that stem from the trauma they faced in Iraq. I am worried that they will simply go from being Iraqi children with problems to Iraqi adults with problems.

I am Syrian, it is my duty to look after my neighbours. My friends and family know that I am doing a hard job. Although I am young I feel their respect for me and my work. ❞

38

What is there to go back for?

Mina Tala was a small child when the war started, and she and her twin brother were terrified by the noise and explosions. Eventually Mina Tala and her family left for Syria, where they are waiting until they feel safe to return.

●● I was six years old when the war started. Even as a young child, I felt the difference when the war started. There were planes in the sky and loud explosions. I was used to playing with the neighbours, but my mother did not allow me to play any more after the war started. In the house there was nothing to do. There was no electricity, so no games. Just long hours of doing nothing and listening to explosions.

My twin brother and I would get scared sometimes and stay as close to our mother as we could. Over time we became used to the sound of the explosions … used to having to stay inside the house all the time.

One day we went to visit my grandmother. When we returned home the front door was broken and the whole house was turned upside down. Even our bedroom and our toys were messed up. I was very scared. The sight of the house in such a mess made us all panic. We did not want to stay in the house with a broken door. My parents sent us to my aunt's house to stay. A few days later we returned home and I tried to help my family tidy up.

Early one morning we woke up and my brother found a letter by the door. My father was still sleeping, but my mother was in the kitchen. My brother gave her the letter and we did not think anything more about it. Now I know that the letter threatened my family, telling them to leave the house or be killed. My mother carried on as usual, preparing breakfast. She did not even wake up my father. I later overheard her saying she was worried that my father should not be woken up with a big shock.

A few days later we left our house. At the time I did not know we were leaving for good. Perhaps I should have known that this was a serious move because I still remember packing every space of the car with our luggage. My parents just told us that we were going to visit our uncle in Baghdad. At my uncle's home I still didn't feel safe – before entering a room I would always worry about a thief being there.

We spent one year with our uncle. We were a little older, so a little less scared by the explosions. I was happy when my parents started talking about leaving for Syria. I wanted to feel safe again. I wanted to be able to play again. I miss my friends, I miss my cousins, but now that I am older I would have two important questions for my parents before returning to Iraq, 'Why are we returning?' and 'What has changed?' ●●

Above *Mina Tala and her twin brother Mustafa paint pictures showing how they were driven from their home.*

Right *Mustafa's painting, Becoming a Refugee.*

A Lost Childhood

In the early 1980s, Saddam pushed an agenda to improve the education and health situation in Iraq. His literacy programme was compulsory; those that did not participate risked time in prison.

Hundreds of thousands of Iraqis learned to read in the years following the initiation of the programme, and by 1990 Iraq was considered to have one of the highest literacy levels in the Middle East. At this time Iraq ranked near the top of virtually every indicator of human well-being – infant mortality, school enrolment, family food consumption, wage levels and rates of employment. The United Nations Educational, Scientific and Cultural Organisation (UNESCO) even gave Saddam an award for his part in eradicating illiteracy in Iraq.

Right *Bilal, an Iraqi child, painted this portrait of the famous Iraqi poet Al Khawezmi.*

Nearly two decades of wars and economic sanctions resulted in schools falling into disrepair, enrolment dropping and literacy levels falling. Since 2003, the war has resulted in thousands of teachers fleeing Iraq, leaving schools understaffed and depressed.

Despite these setbacks, Iraqis continue to be proud of their education system, and many Iraqi refugees have taken their children on visits back to Iraq just so they can take their exams there.

A teacher worries about her children

Safaa is the headmistress of a home-based school in Syria, which helps Iraqi refugee children keep up with their education. She loves her job, but worries about the future for her young pupils.

●● We know that it is hard for Iraqi refugee children studying at Syrian schools – an entirely new education system – so we support them with after-school classes. Almost all the Iraqi children I know are dealing with problems that result from their experiences in Iraq. My own children were not spared. They saw their home destroyed and suffered the terror of fleeing to a foreign country. We are safe today, but one of my children still shakes. The other stutters. Our every waking moment is a reminder of the terror we escaped.

Amongst the children at my school I would say that there are two categories. There are those who are happy that they left Iraq. They were trapped in their homes, unable to play outside, unable to go to school. Here they are free

Above *Safaa feels good knowing she is helping prepare young Iraqis for the future.*

Right *Some children were too young when they left to remember Iraq, but others miss their old schools and their friends.*

and safe. The second group was devastated to leave home. They miss their friends, their homes and their relatives. Some people say that we are lucky to have oil in our country, but I believe that oil is a curse for us. It did not bring anything good for us. If there were no oil, there would be no misery, no war in Iraq.

I can tell you that the greatest strength of Iraq is its people. The Iraqi people value education above everything. For generations, Iraqis have built an education system that we came to depend upon. Everything was free.

As a teacher, a mother and a wife, the war in Iraq has damaged my

home, my profession and the future of Iraq. I believe that we are at an extremely important moment when we have the opportunity to regain our strength. Nearly all those people left in Iraq are professionals. There is still time to save this situation if Iraq can become safe enough for us to return to rebuild our homes, educate our children and learn to live together again. We cannot do this alone. It is much more difficult to build peace than wage war, but we Iraqis are strong and believe in our country. If you support us while we are refugees and when (one day I hope) we return, we will help to rebuild an Iraq that we can all live with. **99**

Left Iraqis consider education to be very important, so they welcome the help offered by community-based schools like the one run by Safaa.

A clown from Iraq

Seif is a clown. He loves making people laugh, but he discovered that this was a dangerous occupation in Iraq.

❝ I come from a family of artists and poets. They were happy for me when I decided to study Theatre at the Faculty of Arts. Their happiness, of course, did not anticipate a war that would turn our values upside down. Shortly after starting university I joined the Happy Family clown troop. We were hired by a foreign circus troop to support their show. It was my first big show. I was so happy with my work, I ignored the war raging around me.

The day after the first show Happy Family received a threat: 'Stop working with foreigners or you will be killed.' Our director held a meeting and gave us the choice – continue or quit. We all decided to stay. One week later our rehearsal space was attacked in the night with a sound bomb. The set was ruined.

The foreign clown troop left and we hoped that their departure marked the end of our troubles. We rehearsed day and night for a new show to celebrate the Day of the Child. The first day of the show was very hectic. Two of our troop had gone to get supplies for the show, and when they didn't show up later we started worrying. They were not answering their phones. The theatre was full of children, so we had to go ahead and perform without our colleagues.

At the end of the show the director walked on to the stage to stop the applause. He had terrible news. Our two colleagues, two of our best clowns, had been killed. This was the end of our Happy Family. The director left for Egypt. His brother, my friend Rahman, tried to join him, but was turned away at the airport.

I carried on studying at university and landed a part in a comedy show for Iraqi television. Every episode I would play a different role – doctor, politician, teacher, nurse. I made people laugh and I regained my happiness.

But in March 2006 I received a threat to quit the show or be killed. The threat was a hand-written note with three bullets inside, just in case I doubted their intentions. I carried on performing. What else can an actor do? In June I was with my uncle and aunt in their car when another car blocked our route. It was like a movie. Four masked men in the car shot at us. My aunt and uncle jumped to cover me. They were both shot. I was in such shock I passed out. In hospital I was desperate to find out what had happened to my aunt and uncle. The doctor told

Above *Seif came from an artistic family and always wanted to perform. As a clown, he gets great pleasure from making people laugh.*

Right/Below *While the adults tell their stories to workers at the UNHCR centre in Syria, Seif and his clown friends entertain the children.*

me they were recovering at home. My family would not let me go home when I was released from hospital so I went to stay with my grandparents. There was a weird atmosphere – no one would tell me anything. My father came to visit to tell me he had sent my resignation to my employers.

I was going mad staying in the house all the time so one day I walked out and went home. When I arrived my father told me, 'Your aunt and uncle were killed. It was because of you they died. We have to take you out of Iraq.'

I left Iraq with my friends Rahman and Ali. I did not say goodbye to my family. I have since received word from my parents that I should not come back.

Arriving in Syria was not easy. None of us had any family to turn to. We were on our own, with only our red noses to keep us happy. They were our security and our future. We started to try to find work with children. A few

birthday parties helped us pay the rent. Then the UN Refugee Agency heard about us. They had hired an international clown troop for World Refugee Day and had seen the positive effect clowns could have on refugees. We were hired to work every day at the UNHCR registration centre and at community centres where Iraqi refugees go to ask for help.

Today our days are packed with performances. Every day we meet

new Iraqi children. I rarely hear their stories but I see their nervousness and their sadness. I feel proud that we make children happy on days when their families are asking for help and telling their stories of sadness. It is not easy for children to hear their parents talking about this. Although I know that nothing will take away these sad stories, I hope that my work helps these children regain their happiness and calm. 99

Saying goodbye

In a continuation of Adam's story (see page 34), he describes how the situation became unbearable and his family decided to leave Iraq.

●● My parents told me three days before our departure that we were going to leave. They had been planning to leave ever since my brother was nearly kidnapped outside school. The situation in my neighbourhood became impossibly dangerous. The main street in the neighbourhood became known as 'death street'. Our house backed on to this street. The back wall was peppered with bullets. For months my mother had been too scared to put the laundry in the garden, so our house was full of laundry at all times.

I had one suitcase to fill, while my bedroom was full of my childhood memories. It was hard to choose what to take and what to leave. I was not allowed to tell

Adam looks out over the rooftops from his new house in Syria. Although he feels safe here, he doesn't feel like this is his home.

anyone that I was leaving The hardest thing was to say goodbye to my friends and neighbours. The war had made us so close. I had friends from the next three streets. Over the summer we had formed teams according to our streets. We could not play football on the street so we played football on the Playstation. I was on the Sparks team. Another team, the Hotcakes, was winning, but I was a star member of my team. All summer long we played this game, and now I was leaving – leaving my team and the best friends I could wish for.

The evening before our departure my friends had a dinner for me. We had a barbecue in the garden. This was the best party I have ever had. After the party they came to my house to help decide what to put into my suitcase. In the other rooms of the house my father had his friends, my mother

> **The hardest thing was to say goodbye to my friends and neighbours.**

her friends. All were helping to make these difficult decisions. All the important things that could not fit into suitcases were given to my aunt.

We left very early in the morning. Our family and friends were on the street to say goodbye to us. We all felt sad that most of our friends did not know we were leaving. It was too dangerous to tell a big group of people – it put us at risk of being robbed by militia en route to the border. But

everyone knew we had no choice. I understood how my friends who had left before me must have felt. All through the year desks suddenly became empty, homes locked up, as my friends left for Syria and Jordan.

Our driver knew what he was doing. He drove at 160 km an hour the whole way to the border. Our only stop was at a checkpoint in Baghdad. The guard asked my father about the names of us kids. We became scared

Left *Despite the upheaval of the flight to Syria, Adam is determined to keep up his education. He has applied to a number of universities in the US and has been told that he has a good chance of being accepted with a scholarship.*

after he walked away, worried that perhaps he would take Omar. Poor Omar was terrified in the back seat. My father made a snap decision and ordered the driver to leave as quickly as possible. We drove off at high speed from the checkpoint and did not stop until we reached the Syrian border.

Arriving in Syria was a relief and a shock. We were in a foreign country with no friends or neighbours around the corner to welcome us. We took the first apartment we found. I had never entered such a poor home before, and now it was *my* home.

Three weeks later the rest of my father's family followed. They arrived in terrible shape. Their driver had also driven very fast and had an accident on the road. The baby was thrown across the car and was bruised all over. Luckily no one died. ●●

Minorities in Iraq

Iraq's minorities, some of the oldest communities in the world, have been driven from the country by a wave of violence against them. The power vacuum following the invasion of 2003 allowed these minorities to be targeted for reasons such as being "unbelievers" or because they identified or shared religions with Western countries. They have been targets of kidnappers because they are thought to be rich and to have no militia or tribe to protect them.

Above and Right *A school in Al Tanf camp, on the border between Iraq and Syria, for Palestinian refugees.*

Many Iraqis who belong to minority faiths in Iraq have been targeted by religious fanatics. Despite widespread reports of improved security in Iraq in 2008, for example, tens of thousands of Christians were systematically driven from Mosul by militias. Sabean Mandeans are traditionally jewellers and goldsmiths, and this has made them attractive targets for abduction. The Yezidi, their religion shrouded in secrecy, have been targeted both for their religion and for their territory in northern Iraq. Amongst the worst-affected minorities is the 35,000-strong Palestinian community in Iraq. Many have been in Iraq since 1948, with no hope of returning to their homes in Palestine. No country welcomed them when they attempted to flee Iraq.

"Iraq's non-Muslim religious minorities – particularly Christians, Mandeans and Yezidis – have suffered religiously based attacks and other abuses, and have fled the country, at rates far disproportionate to their numbers, seriously threatening these communities' continued existence in Iraq."

The US Commission on International Religious Freedom Report on Iraq, December 2008

Left *Guests at a wedding celebration in the Al Tanf camp.*

Shehab's story

Twelve-year-old Shehab's grandparents fled Palestine in 1948. In 2003 his brother was murdered and he and his family left Baghdad, where the militia was threatening thousands of Palestinians. He describes himself as a triple refugee, never having received citizenship in Iraq, then living secretly in Syria and now in no-man's land between Syria and Iraq.

66 I live in a refugee camp between the borders of Syria and Iraq. My brother was killed on the street in Baghdad. He was stopped by the militia who asked for his identity papers. When they saw he was Palestinian they killed him on the spot.

Right *Shehab is a Palestinian child born in Iraq. He feels he and his people are not welcome anywhere.*

We heard the camp was bad, but nothing prepared us for this hell on Earth.

My family tried to flee Iraq but no country would take us. We crept into Syria with false passports, but after one year of worry, watching our friends and family being arrested and deported to this camp, my father decided he would rather go voluntarily than be humiliated.

We heard the camp was bad, but nothing prepared us for this hell on Earth. On one side there is a motorway, just metres from our tent, with no wall to protect us. A few days after I arrived, a young boy was killed by a truck. For a few weeks I stopped playing football, but this is my greatest pleasure in life, so I started again.

Since I came to this camp, I have been overwhelmed by the smell of the place. When it rains the water sloshes down from the motorway into our tents, inundating the place with water and sewage. Our neighbours are rats, scorpions and snakes.

Right now it is winter and it is bitterly cold. We use a generator to power the electric heaters in our tents. A few weeks ago one of our neighbours died after her tent caught fire in the night. She was pregnant. Her poor husband is devastated.

Even in this terrible place there are good parts to my life. My hobbies are football and drawing. I like to draw my memories of good times in Iraq. I also draw pictures of my life in the camp. It helps me to make sense of my life.

One day I want to be a professional football player. The adults in the camp do not like us playing football. The rule is that if the ball goes on to the road, an adult has to get it. This can make a game very slow. Even though my school is in a tent, I am

Above *Shehab took this photograph of the refugee camp that is his home.*

getting a good education. The people in this camp are all well educated and many of them teach us.

I go to sleep at night thinking about dying. Am I going to get burnt tonight? I find it very difficult to relax and all my worst memories are relived during the

I go to sleep at night thinking about dying. Am I going to get burnt tonight?

night. The morning comes as a huge relief to me. I can go to school, play with my friends, and stay out of the tent.

My parents tell us stories about our first home in Palestine and our second home in Iraq. I only dream of where my third home will be, where I can live under a roof, safe and welcome. ❥❥

A Sabean child

Saja comes from a Sabean Mandean family. The origins of Mandeanism date back around 2,000 years to Mesopotamia, in modern-day Iraq. Estimates suggest there are only 70,000 Mandeans left today worldwide. Mandeanism is a religion that preaches and practises peace – it bans killing or bearing arms under any circumstances. As a result they have been unable to defend themselves against violence.

●● From the day my sister was taken, my childhood ended. My parents and six brothers and sisters were with me at home when gangsters charged into our house. They were wearing black masks. They knew who my father was, telling him, 'We know you are a goldsmith, we know you are hiding gold. Hand it over or we will kill your whole family.' The men became very angry and beat my father. They put us children in another room and we cried with terror.

Then they came into the room and pulled out my beautiful sister Maha. My father yelled at them, 'Stay away from my daughter!' but they taunted him that they were going to take her and marry her. We are Sabean Mandean and our religion does not allow us to

"We know you are hiding gold. Hand it over or we will kill your whole family."

Left Saja and her mother, who spend most of their day at home, waiting for a better future.

marry someone outside our faith. If we do, we are rejected. The men yelled, 'You are unbelievers, we will take all of your children!' They left the house, with my sister screaming and crying.

My father has searched for my sister. Our friends have searched. We have never heard from her again. Since this time many of our friends have married their children very young to protect them, to keep them in the faith.

We fled to Syria soon after, where we feel much safer. Even so, I am afraid to go out. I have no desire to go to school. I just want to stay safe with my family. I don't believe I will ever be safe again in Iraq. All I want is to live in a safe country where we can work and build our future. We wait every day hoping for a call from UNHCR to tell us that a country has agreed to resettle us. We queue up regularly outside the offices to find out if there is any hope. Until another country welcomes us, we will continue to live in limbo. ❝❞

A young married couple from the Sabean community who married early as a protection.

Forced from Mosul

Sara and her mother are Christians who have lived in Mosul all their lives. In October 2008 there was a mass exodus of Christians from Mosul when they were threatened by the militia. Tens of thousands fled to the villages surrounding the city, and to the Kurdish areas in northern Iraq. Only those that managed to secure a visa were able to flee to Syria and Turkey.

Sara holds up her identity card, which put her in danger in her last days in Iraq.

"I was at work when one of my colleagues received a threat on the phone telling her that all Christians should leave immediately or be killed. My colleagues wept as all the Christians in the office rushed out of the building.

I came home to my mother and we stayed at home for two days, but the situation was terrifying. We heard that 11 friends had been killed at checkpoints by militia dressed as police. We heard that they were killed on the spot after their identity cards were examined and showed them to be Christians.

A car passed by our house with a loudspeaker shouting that we should leave or be killed. My mother and I packed immediately and put on veils and traditional Islamic dress to hide our identities. We took very minimal luggage, so we wouldn't draw attention to ourselves. We took the money that we had hidden in the house. A trip to the bank was too dangerous.

Eleven friends were killed on the spot after their identity cards were examined and showed them to be Christians.

We were lucky that we had visas for Turkey. A few weeks earlier the first threats had worried us and we had applied for these visas. Syria is en route to Turkey, and we felt that this was our safest option. We had spent Christmas in Syria in the Christian village of Seydnaya. In this part of Syria, Aramaic, the language of Christ, is still spoken, and we felt that we had the best chance of finding peace and solidarity there.

We arrived in Seydnaya feeling very lonely and vulnerable. We met some other Iraqi refugees, who helped us find an apartment. They brought us to UNHCR to ask for help. After our meeting with UNHCR we have a refugee certificate and a date when we can collect food, mattresses and blankets to see us through the winter.

Since we arrived in October we have met up with members of our church who have also fled the violence in Mosul. We are all waiting in Syria, not really sure what to do next. We do not have the right to work in Syria. We are scared to return to Iraq. None of us ever thought we would leave Iraq, but now we are wondering if we will ever be able to return."

Right *A newly arrived child waits at a church in Seydnaya while his mother finds help.*

Poverty

Many Iraqi refugees left in a great hurry, their lives threatened both by the general level of insecurity and targeted threats.

We Don't Have Any Money Left
by Fatima Waleed.

Before leaving, the refugees tried to gather their savings and sell belongings and property in order to survive in the future. This provided yet another opportunity for criminal gangs, who became expert at identifying departing families and robbing their last belongings before they left.

The majority of refugees chose to settle in the regional capitals, with over 60 per cent fleeing Baghdad. In Damascus, capital of Syria, several areas began to take on a distinctly Iraqi atmosphere, with Iraqis of all religions choosing to live together. The markets in these areas feature Iraqi bakeries, fish shops and restaurants.

Government policy in Syria was to welcome the Iraqis as their guests – this is part of Arab hospitality. As with all refugees in Syria, Iraqi refugees have not been given the right to work, though. As a result they are entirely dependent on the savings they brought from Iraq, the help of family and friends and support from aid organisations.

As the savings of the refugees have run out they have found themselves in situations of unimaginable poverty. The worst consequences of this policy are homelessness, child labour and even early marriage for young girls so that there is one less mouth to feed.

Working for survival

Twenty-year-old Mustafa tells his story of survival and hardship, feeling betrayed by both his father and his countrymen.

❝ I cannot pretend that my life was perfect before the war. My father was abusive, we all suffered, my mother, my sisters and I. But we had my mother's love, a home, and were progressing with school. My mother dreamed that I would become a doctor. I'm not sure I would have made it because my father's violence interfered with my life, but I felt I had a chance.

This all ended one day in 2006. I walked to school with my best friend, Omar. Outside the gates we were met by militias. First they asked Omar his name. When he told them, they shot him three times instantly. I was next. I told them my name and the next thing I felt was a sharp blow on my head from a gun. I don't know why they didn't finish the job. They ran into the school, found the headmaster and shot him. What do we all have in common? We all have the bad luck that we come from Tikrit, home of Saddam Hussein.

I held my dead friend in my arms until schoolmates carried me away to hospital. When my parents arrived I fell apart. I did not want to leave. I cried for the first time in years and then lost consciousness. My parents insisted on taking me home.

Two days later a threat arrived at our door. It was handwritten with my name on the envelope. Before we even opened the envelope we could feel the outline of a bullet inside. My father banned me from attending school. I think this was the final straw for my mother.

Shortly after, we left my father behind and fled to Syria. We arrived with almost nothing, and suddenly I became the man of the house. I have not had a chance to return to school. I have been too busy working to pay the rent. We rely on the UN for food. At the moment I am unemployed. My last job was as an assistant for an electrician. I was electrocuted three times, but that is not why I left. The reason I left was that I was never paid. As a refugee I don't have the right to work and my employer knew this. Every day I go out looking for opportunities to work so I can bring some money home.

Today I feel that my future has fallen apart. In fact I have no future. I feel a huge responsibility to look after my mother and my sisters. I don't see any hope in life. ❞

Left Adam took these pictures of his friend Mustafa, at home and at work.

Relying on the United Nations

By 2007, the World Food Programme (WFP) and UNHCR had received enough support to offer food assistance to 33,000 people in Syria. Huge queues at the food distribution centres and thousands of phone calls to UNHCR's hotline have since led to constant increases in the numbers of people receiving food, with 127,000 receiving food in 2009. Both programmes are costly, but are essential to stave off the worst consequences of poverty experienced by a refugee population that does not have the right to work.

●● My wife and I are doctors. When we started working as doctors in the 1980s we had a good salary and our profession was a secure and well-respected one. This all changed after the war in 1991. Without warning our oil-rich country was suddenly impoverished. The government over-inflated the currency with a massive printing of cash, and what was a good salary became a pittance; at its worst we were earning US$2 a month.

As doctors, our main concern was always our patients, and they were suffering far more than we were. Most were government workers and were like us – they were living a hand-to-mouth existence that relied on the food distributed every month by the government. That food lasted for three weeks, leaving a week of hunger. Our patients were sick people; seeing them struggle to eat a healthy diet was so painful. I ran a private clinic to help make ends meet, but even this clinic only brought about US$10 a month. And as the years of sanctions went on, our patients were less and less able to pay even a token amount.

The most difficult part about the sanctions was the lack of drugs available. For some reason the government would only send

Left Relying on the UN for Help, *by Aya Mohamed.*

is Sunni, I am Shiite. We really don't know what the difference is. It seemed that militias had two reasons to target us: because we were doctors and because we were a mixed marriage. The final straw was when my neighbour's son was kidnapped. I could not take the risk with my two children, so we fled to Syria.

Today I am living an empty life. I cannot get all the papers I need to work in Syria, so I am at home. My only consolation is my two children, who amaze me with their achievements. They are doing very well at school. I just hope that we can keep this up so that they have the same opportunities I had. ●●

us drugs just before they were due to expire. As a doctor I cannot prescribe out-of-date medicines, so I would send my patients away with an empty prescription.

Everyone became so tired, depressed. For many of my friends their only hope was to leave Iraq. As a doctor this was impossible for me. A law from the government prohibited the departure of any doctor from Iraq. I was a prisoner in my own country.

Above These two doctors are scared to show their identities.

Right Crowds queue for assistance from the UN.

After the fall of Saddam Hussein, life looked up briefly. My salary increased to US$300 a month and we were no longer living a hand-to-mouth existence. But this was short-lived. In 2005, I started receiving threats. My wife

Families Divided

According to a survey conducted for UNHCR in late 2007, 77 per cent of the Iraqi refugees surveyed in Syria endured aerial bombardments, 80 per cent witnessed a shooting, 68 per cent have been harassed by militias, and 75 per cent knew someone close to them who had been killed. Disturbingly, 23 per cent had been kidnapped, 22 per cent had been beaten by insurgents and 16 per cent had been tortured.

With so much violence and persecution, families fled their homes in search of peace and security. As the number of Iraqis leaving their homes reached unprecedented levels, Iraq's neighbours – overwhelmed and concerned about their own stability – started imposing a variety of measures and restrictions on refugees. In some cases, Iraqi refugees have resorted to paying smugglers to help them reach safety, and in other cases Iraqi families are separated by cumbersome visa restrictions.

Many families have been divided during the course of their escape from violence. Some have fled to neighbouring regions in Iraq to become "internally displaced", others to neighbouring countries Jordan, Syria, Lebanon and Egypt. Some have travelled further afield to Europe seeking asylum, while still others have been offered resettlement by Western countries. As a result some Iraqi families are now spread across the world, in contact only by phone and email. Many are unable to obtain visas to visit one another.

Left Mother Alone, by Mina Tala
(see page 39).

Caring for grandchildren in Masaken Barzeh

Ghazala Touma and her husband Yaghob Awaraha are taking care of their grandchildren in Syria after their mother was killed and their father left in search of a better future in Europe.

❝ Our daughter was working as a cleaner for the US forces in Iraq. She was earning a good salary, and this was helping to pay for the children's education. One day after she finished work she was killed. We were devastated. Her children and husband were distraught.

Her death opened our eyes to a situation that we had not really acknowledged properly. We are Christians who have lived side by side with Muslims all our lives. We have always felt respected by our neighbours. It was not that they stopped respecting us, we just felt that there was so much fear and violence that they were avoiding us. With our son-in-law and grandchildren crying and mourning their mother, we took on the role as parents and heads of the family.

We arrived in Syria a devastated family. Our other children gave us extra money, so we were able to rent an apartment. But there is no way that we can compare this small apartment with our old home. We were not able to bring much with us, but we did bring portraits of my daughter, and she looks down on us every day.

Within a month of arriving in Syria my son-in-law was feeling frustrated and worried. He had ambitious plans for his children, but they were not even attending school. He was not allowed to work, so one day he left. We had no idea where he had gone.

Right *With their daughter dead and their son-in-law living in Sweden, this elderly couple have the responsibility of looking after their grandchildren.*

The next six months were hard. The two children were not at school. It was too hard to adjust. We were so worried about their father. In the meantime our son was still in Iraq, and we felt terrified by the accounts other refugees told us about the violence in Iraq. Finally we heard from our son-in-law. He had paid a lot of money to some men who helped him reach Sweden. He said that he hoped he would soon be able to send for us.

We have recently heard the news that our son was shot in Iraq. He will come to Syria as soon as he is well enough to travel. We have so much responsibility, and we do worry. What if something happens to us? We both have heart problems.

The children are at school now. We are grateful that the Syrian government welcomes children. They have lovely smiles, but nothing can mask their sadness. I hope that they are reunited with their father soon. They deserve the best future. ❞

Enough War

The massive insecurity in Iraq resulted in thousands of deaths. Huge demonstrations demanding the end of the war in Iraq contributed to pressure on US and UK governments to find an exit strategy. Many Iraqis blame the invasion for the insecurity in Iraq and the damage that has been caused, but are fearful about what may happen in the future once all troops have withdrawn.

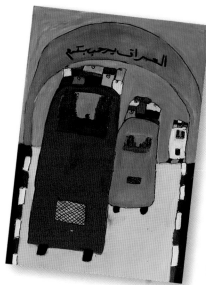

Far Left Normal Life Returns to Iraq *by Sarah Haddawi.*

Left Iraq Welcomes You Back, *by Ali Waleed.*

Right Hello Old Friend *by Aya Mohamed Selman.*

By 12 April 2009, the Iraq Body Count website estimated that between 91,385 and 99,774 Iraqi civilians had been killed by military or paramilitary action. According to antiwar.com, as of 12 April 2009, 4,271 American soldiers have been killed in Iraq since 2003, with an additional 318 coalition troops killed in Iraq during the same period.

The surge

During a speech in January 2007, President George W. Bush announced a major shift in US policy to help stabilise Iraq. The increase in troops (20,000 additional soldiers being sent to Iraq, most of them to Baghdad) became known as the "surge". He expressed a hope that this "surge" of military power would provide the necessary conditions for reconciliation, peace and security for Iraq.

Withdrawal

In December 2008, the British prime minister, Gordon Brown, announced that the British military would withdraw from Iraq by the following summer, with all but a few hundred troops to leave by June 2009. Part of US President Obama's election promises included an exit strategy of US forces. In February 2009, Obama announced that he would withdraw combat forces from Iraq by August 2010, and the remaining troops by December 2011.

Security improvements

By 2008, improved security conditions were widely recognised in Iraq, giving hope for the first time for the country's future. However, deep problems remain in terms of security, living conditions, reconciliation and political progress. Abductions, bombings and shootings continue to hit the headlines on an almost daily basis.

Iraqi refugees living outside Iraq need further reassurance that the situation is safe and welcoming before they can consider returning. In addition, living conditions for large numbers of them remain poor, with many areas suffering from a lack of electricity, fuel, clean water, medical care and employment opportunities. Many refugees lost their homes due to the violence. Others do not feel they can return to areas that are dominated by a different religious sect. Many formerly mixed communities are now divided,

On a positive note, an increasing number are going for quick visits into Iraq, and the majority are in touch by telephone and email with friends and relatives in Iraq. While many welcome the withdrawal of foreign troops from Iraq, they also fear that a new power vacuum will lead to future instability and violence in Iraq.

RESETTLEMENT AS A SOLUTION

Resettlement (when countries offer individuals and families the opportunity to take legal residence in their countries) is an option that many Iraqis hope for, particularly those who do not feel able to return to Iraq. Between January 2007 and November 2008, 16,035 Iraqi refugees departed to the USA. In the last three years, Sweden, Finland, Australia, Norway, France, Belgium, the Netherlands, Germany, Italy, Chile, the United Kingdom, Canada, New Zealand, Denmark, Spain, Luxembourg and Switzerland have also welcomed 6,402 Iraqi refugees. UNHCR estimates that over 50,000 Iraqis still need resettlement.

"Let me say this as plainly as I can ... by August 31, 2010, our combat mission in Iraq will end."

President Barack Obama addressing US troops, February 2009

No place to call home

Shahb (age 17) was at school in Damascus when she gave her account of leaving Iraq. During a phone conversation with her mother later on to check whether the family felt comfortable with Shahb's story being published in this book, her mother described Shahb as the "best judge of the truth that we know".

●● When the war started in 2003 my father was very worried that we were going to be in danger, so we moved to a village outside Baghdad. The next six months were very difficult, and we realised our tolerance for the bombs and insecurity was greater than our fear, so we moved back.

Two years passed and we learned to sleep through gunfire. My brother and I received top marks at school. We tried to keep the same dreams and ambitions that we had before the war, to disregard the war.

Then the war came home. Fortunately we were outside the house breaking the fast with our family during Ramadan. We came back home to find that a mortar shell had hit our home. Our house was badly damaged but we felt lucky. We fixed our house and tried to renew our optimism about life, but the situation went from bad to worse. Suddenly the country was divided by religion. In early 2006 a mosque was blown up hundreds of miles away, and the whole of Iraq turned upon itself. Were you a Sunni? A Shiite? If you gave the wrong answer, you were in danger. In our neighbourhood everyone knew our religion, and it was different from theirs.

The first hint that our luck was running out came when I was sent to the shop nearby to buy some food. As I was walking I noticed a car driving slowly beside me with men wearing masks. Without thinking I ran – ran for my life. The shopkeeper

Above *Shahb works hard at school to build a better future for herself and her family.*

ahead saw my terrified face and prepared to lock the shop. As soon as I was in, he locked the door. I believe he saved my life.

After this, I never felt safe again. My parents decided that we had to move to an area where our neighbours would be from the same religion. We felt such pain leaving our beautiful home, but we told ourselves that this was temporary, like before.

Our new home was in an area where everyone came from the same religion as us, but some of my worst memories are from this place. On my way to school towards the end of the year kidnappers tried to stop the bus. We were lucky we got away.

The final straw was the news that our home had been broken into and occupied. We heard the news from our neighbours. They said that even from outside you could see that the entire house was destroyed. All the years my father had worked to make this beautiful home were lost. He wanted to go to the house, to see for himself his destroyed home, but our neighbours told him he would certainly be killed. With no place to call home, we packed our few belongings and last August became refugees.

Here in Syria we are safe and welcomed. I try not to look backwards. I am a top student at my school and my only focus is on my studies. I intend to make my parents proud. ●●

Salim Salem

Salim has been a refugee for eight years – long before the war in Iraq began. He was driven from his land because he felt unsafe and he was not able to play his music. He felt he had to leave in order for his music to survive. But he longs to go home.

●● It took a long time for me to decide to leave Iraq. I was not allowed to play the music of my people in public, so I played at home, in other homes. I travelled to Basra to learn more about the music specific to the region of southern Iraq. This trip gave my music a tremendous boost of inspiration. Soon my private performances were in great demand; people from Saudi Arabia and Kuwait hired me to play at camps they set up in the desert. I would play and talk, and everyone would appreciate learning more about the history and culture of my people.

My oud [lute] was my only luggage. Within days of arriving in Syria I was out looking for places to perform my music. I had left my country behind, but my music spoke about nothing else. My first concert I started with a piece of music with the title, 'Dying Iraqi Children'. The sanctions of Iraq had turned our country into a third world country where simple diseases killed our children. Even though the subject is sad, most of my music is joyful. Iraqis are strong people and I want my music to inspire them to keep their spirits up. When I play, 'Don't Be Sad Baghdad' or 'My Home Will Remain', Iraqis hear sequences of music that are memories of other music they grew up with. Whatever the religion of the people in the audience, they are brought together with an appreciation of what it means to be Iraqi when you listen to my music.

When the war started in 2003, I hoped that this meant that I could return to my country. But the sound of bombs and the terror that spread across the country was like a muffle to all music. In some places like Basra, musicians either shut up or were killed. Religious extremists made it a crime to play music. During the past year I have seen music blossoming again in Iraq. My people are starting to return home. I am preparing my homecoming music for the day that I can go home, which I hope will be soon. ●●

Salim likes to tell stories with his music, describing a musical picture that takes the listener to a place they have never seen. As a refugee, he feels his music is a patchwork of memories that are lost if he doesn't record them.

Not ready to return

Omar does not wish to return to his country yet. He feels uncomfortable with the religious divide in Iraq, even though he feels safe enough to plan the occasional trip home.

"" My name is Omar. This is a dangerous name in Iraq – a name even my best friends would avoid using in public. My parents have returned to Iraq, both of them to good jobs, and they keep asking me why I am not returning. It is very simple. When I went home a few weeks ago to see my parents I found Baghdad full of walls. My beautiful Baghdad has turned into a dusty, messy city where people are divided. I happen to be lucky that I have the choice to stay in exile or return home. There are Shiite areas, Sunni areas, all with high walls to block the other out. But what if we want to be together? I can't imagine what it is like for the minorities like the Christians, the Sabean Mandeans. There is no area they can call a safe haven.

Left *Omar is not ready to return to Iraq yet. He feels that a darkness still hangs over his country, and will stay a refugee until he feels safe.*

As an artist I consider that my art is a result of centuries of development that started in Baghdad. Baghdad has a place in history as being a capital for all, yet today lots of people are excluded. High walls are cutting into the heart of Baghdad.

With the fall of the Saddam Hussein regime we hoped for change. Before, if we smoked on the street during Ramadan we would be jailed. Today? Same thing, we are jailed.

Before, it was hard to speak with an individual voice. Today? Even the personality of my people has changed. We can't mix, we are scared of each other. It is hard to be close to one another.

I want to return to a secular Iraq. An Iraq where people are not cornered by their religion. Where religion is a personal matter. Iraq doesn't feel like home any more. I am a free man. I am an artist. My paintings are light and dark, just like every person. But I do not want to live in darkness. **""**

Like many Iraqi artists, Omar's paintings reflect his feelings about life as a refugee and the devastation that is happening in his country.

About UNHCR

"Everyone has the right to seek and to enjoy in other countries asylum from persecution."

Article 14 of the Universal Declaration on Human Rights

Governments normally guarantee the basic human rights of their citizens. Refugees are a painful reminder of the failure of some states to provide a safe life for their people, free from violence and persecution.

There are refugees in virtually every country around the world. People become refugees when one or more of their fundamental human rights are threatened or violated, and they are forced to flee. UNHCR is the UN agency responsible for the safety and well-being of refugees and others in need of international protection. UNHCR assists countries that host refugees to ensure their protection.

UNHCR's main role is to make sure that countries are aware of their international responsibility to protect refugees, and that no person is returned involuntarily to a country where they fear persecution. UNHCR provides lifesaving assistance to those forced to flee their homes, such as shelter, medical care, food, clean water and education.

A refugee is not just a "foreigner". You do not choose to become a refugee, nor do you choose the circumstances that drove you to leave your country. Living in exile often means having to depend on the goodwill of others for basic necessities, such as food, shelter and clothing – as well as to feel welcomed in new communities. Often refugees end up

People become refugees when one or more of their fundamental human rights are threatened or violated.

Below Farewell by Hassan Hadawi.

contributing to their new societies in many ways.

UNHCR aims to help refugees find lasting solutions. Voluntary repatriation – return to their original homes – is what most refugees hope for, but this is not always possible. In those cases UNHCR helps people rebuild their lives elsewhere, either in the countries where they first sought asylum or in a third country willing to accept them for resettlement.

By mid-2009 UNHCR was helping over 34.4 million people in 116 countries. 147 states have signed the 1951 Refugee Convention and its 1967 Protocol, which spell out the roles and responsibilities of host countries to protect refugees.

Using this book in school

This book offers many openings for teachers, parents and pupils to gain a better understanding of the lives of Iraqi refugees and the recent history of Iraq. Children and adolescents will look back on the war in Iraq as one of the defining crises of their childhood. Since the majority of the book is written in the first person, teachers and students are encouraged to expand their knowledge and understanding of the lives of refugees by making use of this material in the following ways.

School without walls

Shehab (page 50) was living in a comfortable apartment in Baghdad before the war started in 2003. He had never slept in a tent before he came with his family to Al Tanf refugee camp. In addition to the tent that is now home, he also attends school in a tent. His teachers keep the school open even when there is snow, flooding, sandstorms and suffocating high temperatures. Try to imagine how life would be like in a tent. Perhaps you and your teachers could experience a "school without walls"? Invite your local media and share your experiences with the rest of the school community.

Find out how you can help refugees.

Art, theatre and music

Using the picture painted by a refugee child and Adam's story of saying goodbye to his home and friends (pages 34–35), paint, sing or create a play about how you and your family would feel about leaving your home and country. Create a list of the 10 most important things that you would pack if you and your family had to leave your home to go to another country. Make a list of the parts of your life you would miss most.

His history – your history

Hussam (pages 12–13) was born during one war, was a child during the sanctions of Iraq, and was forced to leave his childhood behind when he fled the war in Iraq in 2006. How does this compare to your own history?

Your dreams

Think about the situation that Maysoon's children Omar and Ali are in (pages 26–27). They had to leave their dreams of education to work to support their families. Imagine that you arrive in a new country as a refugee. Your parents have only a small amount of money with them. What are your dreams today and what would you have to give up to help your family to survive?

Human rights

Yorgos Kapranis (see right), from the European Commission's Humanitarian Aid Office (ECHO) highlights the fact that Iraqi refugees have the same dreams as most Europeans – to live in a country that is secure, free, has good education and career opportunities. For those refugees who will not be able to return to Iraq, resettlement remains a lifeline that needs constant support. Find out from your local authorities how you can contact newly arrived refugees, then write a welcoming letter.

Support refugees

Many of the refugees featured in this book are benefiting from assistance from the UN Refugee Agency, but UNHCR is not receiving nearly as much funding as it needs. A jumble sale, a sponsored walk, a donation of pocket money, collection boxes at school on World Refugee Day (20 June every year) – there are lots of ways to raise precious funds. Plan an event with your class to help raise money.

Glossary

air strikes when bombs are dropped from planes to hit targets on the ground.

civil war a war fought between different groups in the same country.

coalition a group of countries joined by a pact or treaty.

displaced persons people who have fled their homes but remain in the same country.

exile forced removal of a person from their home country.

guerilla warfare fighting by independent groups of soldiers.

humanitarian someone who works to improve human welfare.

insurgency a rebellion to overthrow a government.

militants people who use violence and aggression to fight for a particular cause.

militia civilians who are trained as soldiers but who are not part of the regular army.

reprisal an action carried out in response to an attack during a war.

resettlement when countries offer people the chance to take up legal residence.

sanctions when one country refuses to trade with another because of political differences.

Resources

Children of War: Voices of Iraqi Refugees by Deborah Ellis (Groundwood Books, 2009)

Iraq by Simon Ponsford (Franklin Watts, 2006)

Saddam Hussein and Iraq by David Downing (Heinemann Library, 2004)

The War in Iraq by David Downing (Heinemann Library, 2005)

Transitions – Iraqi Musicians on the Move An album featuring music by three Iraqi musicians including Fadi (page 18) and Salim (page 65), available on iTunes and Amazon.

www.iraqiartinexile.com A website for Iraqi refugee artists.

www.refugeesinternational.org The website of Refugees International, which works for assistance and protection for refugees.

www.unhcr.org/numbers-toolkit/NJN-MANUAL-EN.pdf A toolkit about migration and asylum in the EU for teachers.

Index